BIG WORDS FOR LITTLE PEOPLE

Helen Mortimer & Cristina Tra

Respect

OXFORD
UNIVERSITY PRESS

Unique

Every one of us is different. No one is exactly the same.

Just like our fingerprints!

Wishes

We all have our own ideas and hopes and thoughts. We should never be afraid to say what they are.

Matter

Whether we are young or old, however we look and whatever we believe or think . . . all our lives matter.

Fairness

If we take action together we can make our world a fairer place.

Accept

When we welcome and accept each other and enjoy new things together, our own world grows and does not shrink.

Treat

Remember to treat
everyone you meet
with kindness so
that they feel cared
for and important.

Polite

It is polite to think of those around you and understand what they might need.

Rules

We can respect places and things by following rules.

THROW AWAY YOUR RUBBISH!

PLEASE DON'T TOUCH!

Mine and yours

We all have a body and a life that belongs to us.

We should always be able to say what
we want to share about ourselves and
what we don't.

Speak up

If you hear hurtful, disrespectful words think about what you can say to make a change.

Stinky!

You're stupid!

Ugly!

Who cares about you?

It's all your fault!

What words would you use?

That's mean.

Don't call people names.

You're being rude.

That's not true!

You shouldn't say that.

Be proud

If we are confident, strong and proud of who we are, we can share our stories and learn from each other.

We can enjoy the differences
between us.

Respect

Let's believe in ourselves, respect
each other and look after our world!

Ten ideas for getting the most from this book

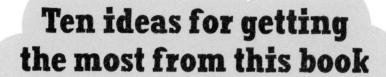

1 Take your time. Sharing a book gives you a precious chance to experience something together and provides so many things to talk about.

2 This book is all about what it means to respect others and to feel respected. What makes you feel important, cared for and respected?

3 It's also a book about language. Ask each other how you would put respect into words.

4 The illustrations in this book capture various moments at a family-friendly festival. We've intentionally not given the children names – so that you can choose your own and perhaps invent something about their personalities. What name would you give to their pet dog? And how can you make sure you respect pets and animals?

5 To fully immerse yourselves in the festival vibe of this book, together

you could choose some songs to create your
own respect playlist and talk about the lyrics
or message of the songs you've selected.

6 Each spread shows a snapshot of respect in action. Why not talk
about what might have happened before and after each moment
that's captured in this book?

7 This book explores respecting others, self-respect
and respecting things and the world around us
– why not talk about how you can bake respect
into what you do every day, even something
like going to the shops?

8 By exploring and recognizing the many different
ways in which we are respectful, we hope this
book will give children and the adults in their
lives the tools they need to make sense of
their feelings and the world around them.

9 Encourage imagination – why not try writing
and illustrating some wishes for your own 'wish
tree' (which could simply be some twigs in a vase)
or making some fingerprint art?

10 You could each choose a favourite word
about respect from the book – it will
probably be different each time you
share the story!

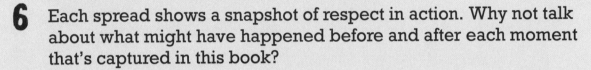

Glossary

disrespectful – if you are disrespectful you
    are rude and not very nice

hurtful – when something is hurtful, it makes you
    feel upset

share – if you share something, you show or tell
    it to someone else

shrink – if something shrinks, it gets smaller

take action – we take action when we want
    to change something
    or solve a problem